D1441756

The Rhine

Europe's River Highway

By Gary Miller

CRABTREE
Publishing Company
www.crabtreebooks.com

Crabtree Publishing Company
www.crabtreebooks.com

Author: Gary Miller
Editor: Barbara Bakowski
Designer: Tammy West, Westgraphix LLC
Photo Researcher: Edward A. Thomas
Map Illustrator: Stefan Chabluk
Indexer: Nila Glikin
Project Coordinator: Kathy Middleton
Crabtree Editor: Adrianna Morganelli
Production Coordinator: Kenneth Wright
Prepress Technician: Kenneth Wright

Series Consultant: Michael E. Ritter, Ph.D., Professor
of Geography, University of Wisconsin—Stevens Point

Developed for Crabtree Publishing Company by RJF
Publishing LLC (www.RJFpublishing.com)

Photo Credits:
Cover: Carola Koserowsky/age fotostock/Photolibrary
4, 6, 7, 10, 12, 18, 20, 21: iStockphoto
8: © mediacolor's/Alamy
11: Wotto/f1 Online/Photolibrary
13: Hendrik Holler/LOOK/Getty Images
14: © Joern Sackermann/Alamy
16: Nicole Gordine/Shutterstock;
17: North Wind Photo Archives/Photolibrary
19: Getty Images
23: Armin Weigel/dpa/Landov
24: Werner Otto/age fotostock/Photolibrary
25, 26, 27: AP Images

Cover: The Castle Stahleck is one of about 30 castles that
overlook a scenic stretch of the Rhine River in Germany.

Library and Archives Canada Cataloguing in Publication

Miller, Gary, 1961-
    The Rhine : Europe's river highway / Gary G. Miller.

(Rivers around the world)
Includes index.
ISBN 978-0-7787-7446-4 (bound).--ISBN 978-0-7787-7469-3 (pbk.)

    1. Rhine River--Juvenile literature. 2. Rhine River Valley--Juvenile
literature. I. Title. II. Series: Rivers around the world

DD801.R74M54 2010   j943'.4   C2009-906243-7

Library of Congress Cataloging-in-Publication Data

Miller, Gary.
  The Rhine : Europe's river highway / by Gary Miller
        p. cm. -- (Rivers around the world)
  Includes index.
  ISBN 978-0-7787-7469-3 (pbk. : alk. paper) -- ISBN 978-0-7787-7446-4
(reinforced library binding : alk. paper)
1. Rivers--Juvenile literature. 2. River life--Juvenile literature. 3.
Stream ecology--Juvenile literature. I. Title. II. Series.

GB1203.8.M55 2010
943'.4--dc22

                                    2009042409

Crabtree Publishing Company
www.crabtreebooks.com   1-800-387-7650

Printed in the U.S.A./122009/BG20091103

Published in Canada
Crabtree Publishing
616 Welland Ave.
St. Catharines, ON
L2M 5V6

Published in the United States
Crabtree Publishing
PMB 59051
350 Fifth Avenue, 59th Floor
New York, New York 10118

Published in the United Kingdom
Crabtree Publishing
Maritime House
Basin Road North, Hove
BN41 1WR

Published in Australia
Crabtree Publishing
386 Mt. Alexander Rd.
Ascot Vale (Melbourne)
VIC 3032

CONTENTS

Words that are defined in the glossary are in **bold** type
the first time they appear in the text.

CHAPTER 1

The Magnificent Rhine

From a distance, the Rhine River and its surroundings look like something from a fairy tale. Thickly forested hills rise from the banks of the river. A stone castle sits on top of a bluff, its towers shining in the sun. Nearby, a village of houses, shops, and church steeples stands in a forest clearing. Beyond the village, vineyards stretch toward the horizon.

The Rhine River is one of Europe's most **economically** and culturally important rivers. From the Alps in Switzerland, it flows 865 miles (1,390 kilometers) through Liechtenstein, Austria, Germany, France, and the Netherlands before emptying into the North Sea. The Rhine River's **drainage basin**, or the area of land drained by the river, is approximately 65,600 square miles (170,000 square km) in size.

From its source in the Swiss Alps, the Rhine River flows north and west along its course to the North Sea.

Early Settlers

People have lived along the Rhine River for thousands of years. Celtic people had settled there by about 700 BC. By 100 BC, Germanic people had settled along parts of the river, too.

Early settlers were attracted to the Rhine River for the same reasons that bring people to the river today. The Rhine River is **navigable**, or able to be traveled by boat, for more than 500 miles (800 km), from the North Sea to Basel, Switzerland. The river serves as a travel route for people and a transportation route for products for trade. People use the water for drinking and to water crops. In the fertile farmland along the river, people grow fruits, vegetables, and grains.

LEFT: The middle section of the Rhine River flows through a scenic valley dotted with quaint villages, castles, and vineyards.

An Important Border

In the past, the Rhine River has been a key military border. Over thousands of years, opposing armies struggled for control of the river and the lands that surround it. Whichever army controlled the Rhine River controlled the transportation along it. The river also provided a protective barrier against attack. Today, part of the Rhine

Portrait of a City: Strasbourg, France

On the French side of the Rhine River, along the stretch of the river that forms the border between present-day France and Germany, lies the city of Strasbourg. It was originally settled by the Celts. Today, it is a major French port that is also linked by canals to the Rhône and Marne rivers. Strasbourg is a center, as well, for education and the communications industry.

This neighborhood in Strasbourg, France, features picturesque half-timbered houses.

River forms the border between the countries of France and Germany.

More recently, the Rhine River has known peaceful times. A treaty known as the Mainz Convention of 1831 made the river an international waterway. People from any nation were free to travel on it. However, this treaty has not always been honored. During World War I (1914–1918) and World War II (1939–1945), Germany, France, and other nations battled for control of Europe. The nations' armies fought fiercely for control of the Rhine River. Today, Europe is at peace, and the river is once again an international waterway.

FAST FACT
Fertile soil along the Rhine River makes its banks an ideal location for vineyards. The region is a top producer of wines.

Cities and Industry

Along the course of the Rhine River lie some of the most economically and politically important cities in Europe. Basel, Switzerland; Bonn, Germany; and Strasbourg, France, all sit on the banks of the Rhine River. These cities grew in

The Rhine River is fed by melting snow and ice in the Alps of Switzerland.

part because of the river's use as a transportation route. The Rhine River carries more commercial traffic than any other river on Earth.

Human use of the Rhine River has seriously damaged this valuable natural resource. For centuries, people have dumped industrial waste, sewage, and other pollutants into the river. By the 1980s, many called the Rhine River "the sewer of Europe." But governments, organizations, and individuals have been working to clean up the polluted waters.

NOTABLE QUOTE

"O, the pride of the German heart in this noble river! And right it is; for, of all the rivers of this beautiful earth, there is none so beautiful as this."

—Henry Wadsworth Longfellow, in *Hyperion* (1839)

CHAPTER 2

From the Alps to the Sea

What force creates a river such as the Rhine? Gravity. First, rain falls from the sky. Some water soaks into the soil, and the excess water flows downhill toward the sea. Small rivulets form and join each other to make tiny streams. Then the streams join and eventually form a powerful river.

Every river follows a unique path, which is determined by the shape, or **topography**, of the river's basin. Both natural and human forces have combined to create the Rhine River basin that exists today. The forces of nature have taken millions of years to do the job. Humans have changed the Rhine basin in less than 200 years.

The Alpine Rhine and the High Rhine

Two streams high in the Alps of Switzerland are the sources of the Rhine River. These **headwaters** join to make the section of the river known as the Alpine Rhine. This fast-moving section flows between Switzerland and two countries, Liechtenstein and Austria, before entering Lake Constance, where the section of the river known as the High Rhine begins. From the lake, the river tumbles about 75 feet (23 meters) over the Rhine Falls.

The Upper Rhine

After passing the Swiss city of Basel, the Rhine River turns sharply northward. This marks the beginning of the Upper Rhine. There the river flows across a broad, flat valley between Germany's Black Forest to the east and the Vosges Mountains of France to the west. Two main **tributaries** join the Rhine River in this section. The Neckar River meets the Rhine River at Mannheim, Germany. At the German city of Mainz, the Rhine River is joined by the Main River.

LEFT: In the Ruinalta, or Rhine Canyon, the river has cut a deep, narrow channel through the forested Alps of Switzerland.

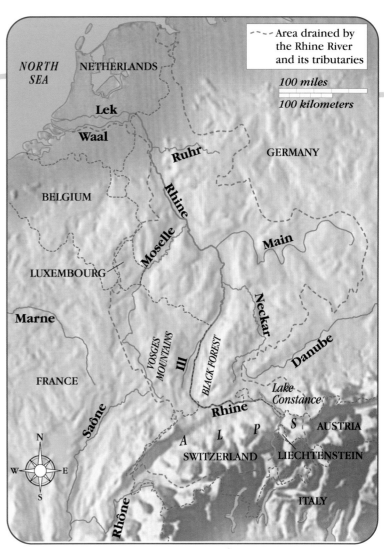

The Rhine River and its tributaries drain a large area of central and western Europe.

The Middle Rhine

Downstream from Mainz is the city of Bingen, in Germany. There the Rhine River drops into a deep, narrow, rock-walled **gorge**, and the Middle Rhine begins. About 90 miles (145 km) long, this section of the river features the storybook castles and beautiful vineyards that draw tourists from around the world. The Moselle River,

The Rhine Falls at Schaffhausen, in Switzerland.

another major tributary, enters the Rhine River at the German city of Koblenz.

The Lower Rhine

After the river leaves the Rhine gorge, the Lower Rhine begins. At Duisburg, Germany, another major tributary, the Ruhr, joins the Rhine River. The Ruhr-Rhine region is one of the busiest industrial regions of the world. A network of railway lines and inland waterways carry goods to the Rhine River. There, ships transport the products to the Atlantic Ocean and around the world.

Farther west, the Rhine River enters the Netherlands. In the lowlands of the Netherlands, the slow-moving river enters its **delta**. There, the Rhine River breaks into two main branches, the Lek and the Waal. Each branch has its **mouth** on the North Sea.

FAST FACT
More than 30 castles, fortresses, and ruins can be found on the banks of the Middle Rhine.

The Ruhr region in western Germany is a major coal-mining and industrial center. A large share of the machinery and other metal products manufactured in Germany are produced in this area.

Geologic Events

Natural forces that shaped the Rhine River include geologic events. About 30 million years ago, forces within Earth shifted huge layers of rock. The layers folded and pushed upward, forming the Alps. In these mountains, the Rhine River has its source. The valley of the Upper Rhine formed when the land between two faults, or cracks in Earth's crust, fell or slipped. This kind of broad, flat-bottomed canyon is known as a **rift** valley.

Human Changes

People have also shaped the Rhine River. Long ago, the Upper Rhine flowed along a winding course. The zigzags meant a long journey for ships traveling along the river. From 1817 to 1874, crews of workers dug channels to straighten the river. This made the trip along the Upper Rhine a shorter one. Engineers also built up the riverbanks to control flooding.

On the Lower Rhine, **silt** carried by the river settles on the riverbed.

A wild boar searches the ground for food. Wild boars live in the Black Forest and in other wooded areas along the Rhine River.

The buildup of silt can clog shipping channels. To prevent this, engineers **dredge**, or dig, the silt from the riverbed. Dredging is a costly task that must be done regularly to keep ships moving.

Woods, Water, and Natural Life

The Rhine River is an important source of drinking water for about 25 million people in Europe. The river also provides **irrigation** water for vineyards, farms, and orchards along its banks, and river water is used by dams to create **hydroelectric** power.

Great forests rise along the river's path. Historically, the woods provided a valuable resource: trees for **lumber**. After trees were cut, many of the logs were floated down the Rhine River to the Netherlands, where they were milled for use in finished products. In the past, so many trees were cut that large areas of the forest were harmed. Today, logging is highly regulated.

Timber Territory

The Black Forest is a center for Germany's lumber and woodworking industries. The forest covers about 2,320 square miles (6,000 square km), and its mountains reach to nearly 5,000 feet (1,525 m). At lower elevations, oak and beech trees grow. Higher up are vast **tracts** of firs.

The forests are home to a variety of plants and animals. Mammals living along the river include beavers, deer, and wild boars. Birds include cranes, coots, and woodpeckers. Long ago, the Rhine River teemed with Atlantic salmon. Pollution eliminated the salmon, but efforts are under way

FAST FACT

The United Nations has named the Rhine gorge a World Heritage Site. To be included on the World Heritage List, a site must have cultural and natural resources that are worthy of protection.

to reintroduce this fish to the river.

The Rhine River basin is not especially rich in other natural resources, although coalfields in the Ruhr region are among the world's largest. Petroleum products, such as oil and natural gas, and metals, such as iron ore and copper, are imported into the region. These products come from various countries, including Brazil, Australia, Saudi Arabia, and the United States.

The Rhine River flows through the Rheingau region of Germany, which is famous for its many vineyards.

13

CHAPTER 3
People Along the Rhine

Since the earliest people had not yet developed a system of writing, the history of the first settlers along the Rhine River is not recorded. But historians say people have lived in the region for thousands of years. The Rhine River has played an important role in the development of human society in Europe, both unifying and dividing cultures and countries.

First Arrivals: The Celts

The first people to arrive were probably the Celts, who settled along the river's upper stretches as early as 700 BC. The Celts were among the first European people to use iron tools. They traded among themselves along the Rhine River. The Celts also traded with people from more distant cultures, including the Greeks and the Etruscans, who formed a powerful nation in central Italy.

By about 500 BC, the Celts living along the Rhine River had developed a culture known today as the La Tené. They produced works of art with complex geometric designs. Eventually, the Celts migrated to Ireland and Scotland, where their culture can be seen today.

Germanic Tribes

By about 100 BC, Germanic tribes had entered the Rhine region, settling mostly along the Lower Rhine. Germanic people included groups such as the Goths and the Vandals. They came to the Rhine region from

Bridge Over the River Rhine

In 55 BC, Roman troops under Julius Caesar built the first known bridge across the Rhine River. The bridge was built of large wooden timbers. Wooden barriers upstream prevented enemies from sending tree trunks down the river to destroy the bridge.

settlements in Sweden, the Danish Peninsula, and northern Germany. Germanic people even crossed the Rhine River to settle in present-day France.

Soon, the Germanic people began to clash with the Romans. The first battles happened in 102 BC, when Germanic armies invaded Roman settlements in present-day France and Italy. Between 58 BC and 50 BC, armies led by the Roman general Julius Caesar gained control of the west bank of the Rhine River.

LEFT: The remains of ancient Roman structures can be seen in Xanten, Germany. A settlement, called Colonia Ulpia Traiana, was founded there by the Romans in about 100 AD.

The People of the Netherlands

For centuries, the Netherlands has been a center of trade and culture. Known as the Dutch, the people of the Netherlands have made great contributions to the world of art. Famous artists from the Netherlands include Rembrandt van Rijn, Jan Vermeer, and Vincent van Gogh. The Netherlands also became an early center of publishing. By the 1600s, it was producing some of Europe's first newspapers.

The Romans

The Romans went on to establish an empire that included much of Europe and parts of northern Africa and western Asia. Roman settlements and trading posts along the Rhine River helped them control their vast empire and trade with people from many

A statue of the composer Ludwig van Beethoven in Bonn, Germany, the city where he was born.

FAST FACT

A settlement existed along the Rhine River at Bonn, in Germany, as early as 1 BC. Today, Bonn is a center of education, the arts, and technology.

different regions, such as Europe, Asia, the Middle East, and North Africa.

The expense of maintaining such a large empire proved too great, however. The Roman government began to weaken. That decline enabled Germanic people to begin to regain control of some of the lands the Romans had conquered. In 410 AD, a Germanic tribe called the Visigoths invaded the city of Rome and partially destroyed it. In 476 AD, the Roman Empire fell. Germanic people once again controlled the land along the Rhine River.

Trade Route Cities

The Rhine River's value as a trade route led people to settle along its banks. Many Rhine tributaries also served as trade routes, so places where tributaries met the Rhine River were the most populated.

The German city of Mainz sits where the Main and Rhine rivers meet. Celts, and later Romans, were among the first settlers in the area. Roman ruins, or building remains, can still be seen there. Today, Mainz is an important center of Germany's chemical industry.

A Place for Printing

Thanks in part to the work of Johannes Gutenberg, Mainz, on the west bank of the Rhine River in Germany, became an early center of printing. In the mid-1400s, Gutenberg invented the process of printing from movable type. The new method enabled people to mass-produce books for the first time.

Johannes Gutenberg

Rotterdam, in the Netherlands, grew from a fishing village into an international port and center of trade and transportation.

Duisburg, at the junction of the Rhine River and the Ruhr River, was chartered as a city in 1129. Today, Duisburg is Europe's largest inland port.

The location of the Netherlands on the North Sea and the country's access to the Rhine River have made the Netherlands an important center for shipping.

In 1890, engineers completed a channel from Rotterdam, a city in the Rhine River delta, to the North Sea. In 2008, Rotterdam was the fourth-busiest port in the world.

The Struggle for Control

For centuries, the French and the Germans battled for control of the Rhine River. Much of the struggle involved a region on the river's west bank known as Alsace-Lorraine. By 1790, France controlled the region. In the Franco-Prussian War (1870–1871), the Germanic nation of Prussia, located mostly in present-day Germany, won control of Alsace-Lorraine. However, at the end of World War I, the region became part of France again.

After World War I, Germany and France built **fortifications** along the Upper Rhine. France constructed a massive network of fortresses, underground tunnels, and minefields called the Maginot Line. The Siegfried line was a series of German defensive fortifications facing the Maginot Line. During World War II, Germany invaded France and **annexed** Alsace-Lorraine. After Germany's defeat in 1945, control of the region once again returned to France. Since then, the region has remained a part of France. Today, France and Germany are peaceful allies, and Alsace-Lorraine is no longer contested.

Occupied Zone (occupied by German military)

Southern Zone

Alsace-Lorraine (annexed to Germany)

After its successful invasion of France in 1940, early in World War II, Germany annexed Alsace-Lorraine, occupied northern and western France, and set up a French government controlled by Germany in the south.

Built between 1930 and 1940 along France's border with Germany, the Maginot Line was meant to protect France against German attack.

CHAPTER 4
Travel and Commerce

Visitors to the Rhine River today find one of the world's busiest rivers. Tugboats push and pull huge barges loaded with cargo such as coal, iron ore, grain, and chemicals up and down the river. At bustling Rhine River ports such as Cologne, Germany, workers use huge cranes to load and unload steel containers packed with goods.

Commerce on the Rhine River is not a new development. In the Middle Ages, the period in Europe from about 500 AD to about 1500 AD, people built castles near narrow stretches of the river. With these fortresses for protection, they blocked access across the river with ropes or other barriers. Sailors who wished to pass had to pay a toll.

A Dangerous Passage

Long ago, trade was not as active along the Rhine River as it is today. Early sailors piloted small wooden boats.

Floods, rapids, and obstacles such as boulders made the Rhine River a dangerous place to sail. Even after steel-hulled steamships were invented, sailors lost their lives on the river.

Starting in the 1800s, engineers worked to make the Rhine River safer and easier to navigate. At Bingen, in Germany, large rocks and underwater **reefs**, or ridges of jagged rock, once blocked the passage of ships. From 1830 to 1832, engineers blasted away many of the obstacles on the Bingen stretch of the river. Later, even more of the rocks were removed.

A barge passes the Lorelei rock on the Rhine River in Germany.

Siren Song

Myths and legends tell stories of the Rhine River. One legend is that of Lorelei. The ghost of a beautiful maiden, Lorelei sang a song that lured sailors to their death on the rocks. The source of the legend is a large river boulder that produces an echo. The rock is called the Lorelei, too.

LEFT: Long barges transport cargo on the Rhine River.

Thanks to the Main-Danube Canal, ships can travel 2,200 miles (3,500 km) from the North Sea to the Black Sea.

Canals

The construction of **canals** increased the Rhine River's value as a trade route by connecting it to other waterways. In 1810, workers began building the Rhine-Rhône Canal. Opened in 1834, this artificial waterway links the Saône, a tributary of the Rhône, to the Ill River. The Rhône River rises in Switzerland and flows south to the Mediterranean Sea. The Ill River flows into the Rhine River near Strasbourg, France. Today, the Rhine-Rhône Canal carries only moderate traffic. A more widely used waterway is the Rhine-Marne Canal, completed in 1853, which also joins the Rhine River at Strasbourg.

Linking the Seas

Completed in 1992, the Main-Danube Canal is only 106 miles (170 km) long. Yet it forms a critical link between the North Sea and the Black Sea, which are about 2,200 miles (3,500 km) away from each other. Ships travel from the North Sea up the Rhine River to the Main River. The Main-Danube Canal then carries them from the Main River to the Danube River. Ships then travel down the Danube River, and from the Danube they can reach the Black Sea.

Canals play a vital role in connecting the Rhine River to ports on the North Sea. The Merwede Canal, built at the end of the 1800s, connects the Rhine River to Amsterdam, an important port in the Netherlands. This canal was enlarged in the 1950s. Its shipping traffic has declined, but the canal is an important waterway for leisure travel.

FAST FACT
About 250 million tons (228 million metric tons) of goods are shipped on the Rhine River annually.

A Commercial Powerhouse

Over the years, the Rhine River has been straightened, and obstacles have been removed. Those improvements have enabled merchants to ship large amounts of goods along the river at a low cost. Shipping goods along the Rhine River is much cheaper than shipping them by truck or even by train. This helped make the Rhine River the most commercially valuable river in the world. Each year, millions of tons of goods are transported on the Rhine River.

Cheap transport of resources has helped to make the cities along the Rhine River a center of the world's chemical industry. One-fifth of the world's chemical products are manufactured along the Rhine River. Among the products made in industrial centers such as Basel, Switzerland, are fertilizers, **pesticides**, and **pharmaceuticals**.

The Rhine River basin is a major agricultural region, too. The region's most important crops are corn, wheat, sugar beets, and grapes.

A barge moves slowly down the Main-Danube Canal in Germany.

CHAPTER 5

Restoring the Rhine

Today, the Rhine River plays a critical role in the economy and daily life of Europe. European businesses depend on the Rhine River as a source of low-cost transportation for natural resources and manufactured products. The shipping, manufacturing, and agricultural industries along the Rhine River provide millions of people with jobs. Dams along the river create hydroelectric power that is supplied to homes and businesses across the region. But the river's major role in supporting transportation, industry, and agriculture has caused serious environmental problems. Today, the governments, businesses, and citizens of the countries along the river's banks are working to restore its health.

Pollution Problems

By the 1960s, the Rhine River **ecosystem** stood at the brink of collapse. Pollutants in the river included waste from chemical companies, pesticides and fertilizers from farms, untreated sewage, and oil leaking from ships. Dozens of species of fish, including the Atlantic salmon, had disappeared from the river. Many plant species had died out, too. Birds and mammals that depended upon the river for food and water also suffered losses. People began working to clean up the river.

Devastating Floods

Flooding also remains a problem along the Rhine River. In 1993 and 1995, floods devastated many communities in the Rhine basin. The main cause of the floods was unusually heavy rain.

Koblenz, at the junction of the Rhine and Moselle rivers, sometimes experiences severe flooding.

LEFT: Power stations on the Rhine River and its tributaries use the force of moving water to generate electricity.

But the changes people made in the river's course to improve navigation made the floods worse.

By straightening the river and building canals, people reduced the size of the Rhine **floodplain**. The floodplain is an area of low-lying ground beside a river. When a river rises, water spreads over the floodplain. Floodplains slow the movement of the water to areas downstream. The loss of floodplains has

FAST FACT
The International Rhine 2020 Program has set goals for restoring wildlife habitats, reducing flood risks, improving water quality, and protecting **groundwater** by the year 2020.

Chemical Disaster

In 1986, a Sandoz chemical plant in Basel, Switzerland, caught fire. As firefighters battled the blaze, 30 tons (27 metric tons) of mercury and other poisonous substances spilled into the Rhine River. More than half a million fish died. The spill was one of Europe's worst environmental disasters.

Firefighters try to put out a fire at the Sandoz chemical plant near Basel, Switzerland, in 1986.

26

Fish ladders help salmon and other fish bypass power dams that are barriers to their natural migration.

New **wastewater** treatment plants have improved water quality. Tighter controls on the handling of chemicals have reduced the number of accidental spills.

People have also worked to restore parts of the Rhine River's floodplain. These efforts have created wetlands that help control flooding. The wetlands also provide **habitats** for plants and animals.

Biologists are working to bring Atlantic salmon back to the Rhine River. The introduction of fish ladders has helped salmon and other fish get past power dams that had prevented their **migration**. A fish ladder is a structure that helps fish move past obstacles. It is usually a series of shallow steps down which water flows. The numbers of salmon living in the river are small, but scientists are hopeful that the salmon population will grow.

worsened the impact of flooding along the Rhine River.

A Brighter Future

Today, the Rhine River is cleaner than it was just a few decades ago. Restricting the release of pollutants has helped clean up the river.

NOTABLE QUOTE

"We really had to get together and clean it up and keep it clean. We realized it could be the death of the Rhine otherwise."

—Manfred Beubler, head of water quality for the Basel region

COMPARING THE WORLD'S RIVERS

River	Continent	Source	Outflow	Approximate Length in miles (kilometers)	Area of Drainage Basin in square miles (square kilometers)
Amazon	South America	Andes Mountains, Peru	Atlantic Ocean	4,000 (6,450)	2.7 million (7 million)
Euphrates	Asia	Murat and Kara Su rivers, Turkey	Persian Gulf	1,740 (2,800)	171,430 (444,000)
Ganges	Asia	Himalayas, India	Bay of Bengal	1,560 (2,510)	400,000 (1 million)
Mississippi	North America	Lake Itasca, Minnesota	Gulf of Mexico	2,350 (3,780)	1.2 million (3.1 million)
Nile	Africa	Streams flowing into Lake Victoria, East Africa	Mediterranean Sea	4,145 (6,670)	1.3 million (3.3 million)
Rhine	Europe	Alps, Switzerland	North Sea	865 (1,390)	65,600 (170,000)
St. Lawrence	North America	Lake Ontario, Canada and United States	Gulf of St. Lawrence	744 (1,190)	502,000 (1.3 million)
Tigris	Asia	Lake Hazar, Taurus Mountains, Turkey	Persian Gulf	1,180 (1,900)	43,000 (111,000)
Yangtze	Asia	Damqu River, Tanggula Mountains, China	East China Sea	3,915 (6,300)	690,000 (1.8 million)

TIMELINE

700 BC	Celtic peoples have settled along the Rhine River.
500 BC	Celtic culture known as La Tené arises.
100 BC	Germanic peoples have settled along the Rhine River.
50 BC	Romans gain control of part of the Rhine River.
476 AD	The Roman Empire falls; Germanic peoples again control the land along the Rhine River.
1817	Straightening of the Upper Rhine begins.
1830	Engineers begin to clear the Rhine River of obstacles at Bingen.
1831	The Mainz Convention makes the Rhine River an international river.
1834	The Rhine-Rhône Canal opens.
1890	Engineers complete a channel from Rotterdam, the Netherlands, to the North Sea.
1892	The Merwede Canal is completed.
1914–1918	World War I is fought.
1939–1945	World War II is fought.
1986	The Sandoz chemical spill devastates the Rhine River.
1992	The Main-Danube Canal is completed.
1993, 1995	Devastating floods damage the Rhine region.
2001	Government officials from nations bordering the Rhine River adopt the Rhine 2020 Program to restore the ecosystem and improve flood protection and groundwater protection.
2008	A wild salmon is found in the Rhine River at Basel, Switzerland; it is the first wild salmon spotted so far upriver in 50 years.

GLOSSARY

annexed Formally incorporated (a region or other territory) within a country

canals Human-made waterways that are used for shipping or irrigation

delta A triangular or fan-shaped area of land at the mouth of a river

drainage basin The area of land drained by a river and its tributaries

dredge To deepen (as a waterway) with a digging machine

economically Related to an area's economy—that is, the way money and goods are produced, consumed, and distributed

ecosystem A complex community of organisms and their environments functioning as a unit

floodplain The flat or nearly flat land along a river or stream or land that is covered by water during a flood

fortifications Structures designed for defense against attack

gorge A narrow canyon with steep walls

groundwater Water within Earth, especially that supplies wells and springs

habitats The environments in which certain plants or animals naturally live and grow

headwaters Streams that form the sources of a river

hydroelectric Relating to electricity that is produced by using the movement of water

irrigation The watering of land in an artificial way to foster plant growth

lumber Wood that is ready for use as a building material

migration Periodic movement from one region to another for feeding or breeding

mouth: The place where a river enters a larger body of water

navigable Deep enough and wide enough for ships to pass through

pesticides Chemicals used to kill insects and other pests that harm crops or other plants

pharmaceuticals Drugs used for medical purposes

reefs Chains of rocks or coral or ridges of sand at or near the surface of water

rift A crack in Earth's crust that widens over time

silt Small particles of sand or rock left as sediment

topography The shape of the land surface

tracts Large areas of land or water

tributaries Smaller rivers and streams that flow into larger bodies of water

wastewater Water that has been used (as in a manufacturing process)

FIND OUT MORE

BOOKS

Foley, Ronan. *The Rhine.* Hodder Wayland, 2005.

Hardyman, Robyn. *Celebrate! Germany.* Facts on File, 2009.

Rees, Fran. *Johannes Gutenberg: Inventor of the Printing Press.* Compass Point Books, 2006.

Aloian, Molly and Bobbie Kalman. *Explore Europe.* Crabtree Publishing Company, 2009.

WEB SITES

International Commission for the Protection of the Rhine
www.iksr.org/index.php?id=58&L=3&cHash=455fdab52c

The Miracle of the Rhine
www.unesco.org/courier/2000_06/uk/planet.htm

River Basin Initiative: Rhine
www.riverbasin.org/index.cfm?&menuid=104&parentid=87

ABOUT THE AUTHOR

Gary Miller is a writer and documentary filmmaker. He has written about everything from burrowing owls and gorillas to wireless technology and wild wolves. Gary has interviewed country music stars, stock car racers, stunt plane fliers, civil rights pioneers, and rocket scientists. When he's not writing or working on a movie, he can often be found kayaking or fly fishing on the rivers of Vermont.

INDEX

Page references in **bold** type are to illustrations.